"Embracing a Spirit of Giving"

KELLY CHRISTINE

WestBow
PRESS
A DIVISION OF THOMAS NELSON

Cover and author photo courtesy of Angela Halterman of Halterman Photography

"Countdown Calendar" illustration by Michael E. Hraba

WestBow Press books may be ordered through booksellers or by contacting:

WestBow Press
A Division of Thomas Nelson
1663 Liberty Drive
Bloomington, IN 47403
www.westbowpress.com
1 (866) 928-1240

ISBN: 978-1-4908-1196-3 (sc)
ISBN: 978-1-4908-1195-6 (e)

Library of Congress Control Number: 2013918442

Printed in the United States of America.

WestBow Press rev. date: 10/30/2013

Contents

To my parents, who instill in me a spirit of giving.

Acknowledgements

I truly believe a family is one of life's greatest blessings.

Thank you to my parents, David and Beverly Klintworth . . . your support, love and faith in me leaves me humbled and honored. The mother I am today is due to the model and example you set for me. This book would not exist without your belief in its vision. Thank you to my siblings, Kevin Klintworth, Lindsay Kissel and Brandon Klintworth. Many of my sweetest memories and greatest laughs are filled with your presence. I am very grateful for each of you.

In addition to my family, there are a few individuals who were directly involved in bringing this dream to life. Thank you to Crystal Day, Danielle Cruz, Dennis Papp, Tristi Carlson and Kim Terashita. Whether it was brainstorming, editing, providing insight, keeping me balanced, or encouraging me along the way, you were a huge asset to this project. Also, a special thank you goes out to my "Circle of Seven" for your continued prayers and friendship.

I am thankful for the family and friends who have walked with me in life and those who travel alongside me today. Some of you encouraged me to write and gave me confidence to share my voice this way. Others have celebrated many joyous moments, braved some of my toughest storms and experienced everything in between. Thank you for sharing this life with me.

To my children Ava Grace, Garrett and Grady . . .

You are the joy of my life and the greatest gift God has given me. As an actress, I have played many roles, but my most meaningful is the real life one of "mommy." I love you dearly and am so proud of who you are and who you are still becoming.

To my Heavenly Father . . .

How do I even begin to thank You for Your constant faithfulness and provision? The phrase "thank you" seems too small and inadequate to frame my words of appreciation. However, being that I am a lover of simple things, these two small words fittingly capture the sentiments of my heart.

In Your Word You say You have a plan for each and every one of us . . . a plan that is good and gives us a hope and a future. Thank You for Your plans for my life and entrusting me with this calling. Thank You for giving me the ability to embrace a purpose greater than myself and helping me connect that purpose with my passion.

I am eternally grateful for the doors You continue to open and the courage You give me to walk through them.

Our Story . . .

It all began on a silent night.

I found myself unable to sleep, staring at the bedroom ceiling at one o'clock in the morning. The room was quiet, lit only by the soft glow of the lights strung along the Christmas tree by the side of my bed.

I played the events of the day back in my mind. The mail had arrived that afternoon with a slew of new ads. I recalled how excitedly my kids flipped through them, tearing the pages with their little hands.

"Mommy, I want this dinosaur! No wait, Mommy, I want this pirate ship! Look Mommy! Look at these building blocks! I want these! Oh, and here's a microphone. I want that too Mommy!"

"Mommy, I want . . ."

That was the phrase I heard over and over again. Their voices rang out in a sweet timbre, but the message underneath struck a discord within me.

I wanted my kids to have Christmas wishes and dreams. However, I couldn't help but think of the true meaning of Christmas and I knew we had lost balance in our home.

What could I do?

I needed to gently turn their eyes in a new direction: toward those around them. Instead of focusing on what they might receive for Christmas, I hoped they would instead find joy in what they could give.

That's when *Embracing a Spirit of Giving* instantly fell upon me.

I can't describe that moment, except to say that was when my silent night became a holy night.

All of a sudden it was there . . .

What if we became a living Advent calendar?

In case you are unfamiliar with this concept, an Advent calendar is a special calendar used to count down the days until Christmas. Growing up, my parents had an Advent calendar in our home every Christmas season.

I grabbed my pen and paper and started writing the different ways to give to others as we counted down each day to Christmas.

The next morning, I laid out my ideas and created a countdown by which our family would give to a specific group of people in simple ways. Then, over the course of twenty-five days, we would show God's love with cups of hot chocolate, homemade decorations and baked goodies. We gave to less fortunate children, seniors, our troops, college students, animals, firefighters, nurses, trash collectors, mail carriers, crossing guards, third-world missions, teachers, children in hospitals, Sunday school teachers, pastors, school custodians, Salvation Army volunteers, friends, the environment, police officers, the hungry and our families . . . all leading to the day when we celebrated the birth of our Lord and Savior.

I wanted to be very intentional in teaching my kids the fruit of giving is really found in the *who*, not in the *what*. They may not have been aware of it, but the time spent making our handcrafted ornaments, cookies, cups of hot chocolate and colored cards required my kids to give something precious and priceless . . . themselves. Thus, we made giving not about *presents*, but about *presence*.

In simple ways, we showed other people they mattered. And for me, that was what Christmas was about. Christ humbled Himself and came to this earth in a crude manger because we mattered. When we gave, we shared the love of Christ radiating from within us.

Ava, Grady and Garrett donating their weekly allowance.

A Few Things I Learned During the Countdown

It is more blessed to give than to receive.
Acts 20:35

I kept a journal during our countdown and faithfully wrote in it every day. When I thumbed though my accounts and reflections, I saw how this countdown inspired me and my kids to grow. The act of giving allowed us to love in simple and practical ways. However, it also gave us the opportunity to examine our motives and challenge our perceptions.

We were blessed by the reactions of those to whom we gave gifts. It's hard not to feel good when a person standing before you is just beaming with joy! Ultimately—for me—the greatest blessing came from what I learned.

I am writing from the heart of a mother and my story is based on the experiences I shared with my children.

Here are a few truths I learned.

It Works

I've heard it takes around one month to form or break a habit. One of my intentions for this countdown was to remain consistent with our giving. That's part of why I loved the time frame of twenty-five days. Without them even realizing it, I was directing my kids to shift their focus in subtle ways. Remaining consistent was like having a steady stream of goodness flowing into our souls. From there, the goodness took root and became ready and available for us to draw upon.

At first, you may find you need to really focus on giving. Eventually, it will become a bigger part of your daily routine. You'll start to shift the way you see the world around you. Perhaps you tend to glance at the tabloid headlines while waiting to check out at the grocery store. One day you may find yourself standing in line and discover that the bold statements that once caught your eye have faded to the background. What stands out now is a small box of breath mints. You know, the one that is your friend's favorite. So, you follow the internal prompting and buy the item. Just think how special your friend will feel when she realizes you not only thought of her, but acted upon that kind thought!

When I first introduced this idea to my kids, I have to admit I was a bit nervous. My kids have generous hearts, but I wasn't sure if they could sustain generosity for twenty-five days. At that time, they were four, six and eight years old. My youngest was in preschool, and the other two were in school full time. Would they burn out? Would *I* burn out?

What surprised me the most was they never grew tired of it.

I was a little fearful the kids would grow weary of the daily making, baking and giving. I half expected to hear them to say, *"Again?"* when I told them our plans for the day. I was wrong. Their excitement surprised me, and I was so proud of the attitude they portrayed.

We have an Advent calendar made up of twenty-five boxes. Typically, I would put a piece of chocolate within each box. This time, in an effort to embrace this season of giving, I decided to also place a rolled up piece of paper that revealed who we were giving to that day. I knew going into this my kids would be excited to open their boxes because they really wanted the chocolate. Regardless, I told myself we were sticking with the plan.

At the beginning of our countdown, every morning was fairly similar: the kids would come stampeding down the stairs, practically knocking each other over. Racing into the kitchen toward our Advent calendar, once voice would proclaim,

"It's my day! It's my day!" Oh, they were so excited! They just couldn't wait—to eat their piece of chocolate.

On the tenth day of our countdown, the moment I had been waiting for finally happened. I heard the familiar *thud, thud, thud,* but this time it was accompanied by Ava exclaiming, "Quick, Garrett! Let's see what we're doing today!"

That was the day giving trumped chocolate.

As a parent, I just want to get it right. I look at the precious faces of my children and see them as gifts that have been entrusted to me. Some days I feel like I've done okay, but then there are others when I wish I could have a do-over. I try to monitor what they are exposed to, who they surround themselves with, what environments they are in, and what they are learning in those places. I want to do all I can to best equip them so they can make good, sound decisions and moral choices.

I knew we were changing the lives of others, but what about the lives of my children? Would the truths I wanted so desperately to take root in their hearts find fertile ground? Would they stick? Or, was our giving a fleeting moment that only existed for a season? Would we find ourselves, a year later, in the same place, coming back full circle to *"I want"*?

I am happy to say it worked.

Now, I'm not going to pretend that there wasn't any excitement over the arrival of the following season's ads. They are kids who get excited about receiving gifts, especially for Christmas. And I'm okay with that. As I pleasantly found out that following year, our balance had become much stronger. We entered into another season of daily giving quite well and continued to make new discoveries about others and ourselves.

I remember how happy I felt when my daughter looked up at me and said, "Giving is fun!" We were at a food pantry. Ava had brought along a dollar with her, so she could buy a cookie later. However, after our tour guide explained how one dollar provided twelve to fifteen meals for a hungry child, she took her dollar from her pocket and gave it to the gentleman.

Today, I can tell you this countdown changed my kids' outlook. Their eyes are more in tune with other people and their needs. For example, we now keep a box of granola bars in our vehicle. When we travel to Nashville, we usually pass a person in need holding a cardboard sign asking for help. Instead of merely staring at him, or diverting our eyes, we are able to show him a bit of kindness and wish him well.

Oh, and the best part about giving a granola bar? It was the kids' idea.

No Strings Attached

I love wrapping gifts . . . love it! After carefully encasing a gift in paper, I used to tie ribbons around it, or make some sort of fancy bow to place on top. However, during our second countdown of daily giving, I stopped tying ribbons to gifts. What happened was that the kids and I were constructing ornaments for our neighbors, when one of them piped up, "We should make a tip jar."

Whoooooah . . .

"A tip jar?" I asked. "And what would the tips be for?" I continued in a tone that implied I knew exactly what the tips were for.

"Ummm . . . never mind," came the sheepish reply.

This little exchange got me thinking.

Do we expect something in return for giving?

I remember getting upset once when I gave a gift to someone and they didn't say "thank you". *"How rude!"* I thought to myself.

Later though, I was more upset with my own internal reaction than I was with the lack of thanks. I had to take a good look at my motives for giving and make sure I had the right intentions. The act of giving should, on its own, be satisfying enough to our hearts. If the gift has conditions to be received, then it was never freely given.

I needed this self-check. Now, when a gift leaves my hands and enters those of another, it is theirs to receive without any conditions. I do not ask for a gift in return, look for acknowledgement, recognition or even a thank you.

So, when you receive one of my packages, don't let my simple wrapping confuse you. For the lack of adorning ribbons is my way of saying, "It's yours."

Simple as that.

No strings attached.

I Took it for Granted

The day we gave to the hungry is the day I learned a hard truth about myself.

Each week before heading to the grocery store, I look through our refrigerator and pantry and check the expiration date on items. If an item has expired, then into the trash it goes and a replacement is placed on my list.

While at the grocery store:

If there is something we need, I put it in my cart.

If there is something I want, but don't necessarily *need* . . . I still pop it into the cart.

If we don't finish the food placed on our table, I wrap it up. More often than not, however, we don't eat the leftovers and down the garbage disposal they go.

However, during that day of giving, it struck me that the items I so casually toss aside could have been a full meal for a less fortunate person.

Ugh.

Well, needless to say, I had some work to do in this area.

The thought of any person, especially a child, going hungry breaks my heart. I can't imagine how that must feel.

When we focus on ourselves, we don't always see what we're doing. However, when we direct our attention to other people, we are able to see ourselves more clearly.

During our countdown, I intentionally focused on having my kids give to other children. Being able to identify with kids their own age was a strong form of motivation throughout the countdown. It allowed my kids to better understand and embrace each daily give. They were floored when they found out that some kids don't eat for days at a time. My goodness, if my kids don't get an afternoon snack, they'll groan about how they're *starving . . .*

Another example is when I told them some children spend their Christmas in a hospital. My kids are usually pretty compassionate when they hear someone is ill. However, knowing there were other *kids* in hospitals resonated with them for the first time that day. I explained to them that for some kids, the four walls of a hospital room are more familiar than those of their bedroom back home.

They could not believe that some kids had to celebrate Christmas in a hospital. So, we came up with the idea of making Christmas decorations and decorating the pediatric wing of our local hospital.

We found a cute template for paper wreaths and got to work. Garrett had a bit of trouble cutting his construction paper and thought his wreath didn't look as nice as the rest of ours. I assured him it was great and off we went.

We arrived at the hospital and made our way to the elevator. At that moment, Garrett reached up and tightly grabbed my hand. "Do you think they'll like my wreath?" he asked with hopeful eyes. "I tried my best to get it right." I swear, I almost started sobbing in the lobby! "They are going to love it! I love it!" I barely choked out.

After making our way to the pediatric wing, we were greeted by a friendly nurse. Ava and Grady ran up to her with their wreaths. Garrett, however, stood behind me with one hand clutching my leg. I beckoned her to come over as I knelt down beside my son. "This is a special wreath for a very special child," I told her. She held my gaze with an understanding look and said, "I know just the boy." Garrett beamed!

As we left the hospital, I told my kids how proud I was of them. But then, Ava asked why we couldn't meet the kids there. I explained that hospital policy did not allow us to do so, which I completely understood. However, a few days later, we received an envelope from the hospital. In it was a touching note from the boy and his family thanking Garrett for his "cool and awesome wreath."

I think it was good for my kids to not only hear me talk about children in hospitals, but to actually go there and experience it. As I said earlier, they could identify with giving to children their own age. Although the children in the hospital could not be home for Christmas, our visit gave us the chance to show love, put a little more joy in their season and, at the very least, let them know people were thinking about them.

This project revealed to my kids and me some of the privileges we take for granted. It also convicted us to make some changes and become better stewards with what we have been given. Now we know we are not entitled to things just because we want them. We are more grateful for what we have and show God's love for all people by using our resources to help those in need.

It's the Simple Things

Those close to me know of my love for hot chocolate. They are my *cups of good cheer.*

I admire volunteers who stand outside various stores, ringing a bell for charity. We used to live in the Chicago area in Illinois. Trust me, there is a reason why it's called the "Windy City." When the temperature drops, that cold wind can be brutal! Watching a volunteer clasp his scarf in one hand, while wishing passers-by a "Merry Christmas" through chattering teeth is very moving.

So, one year, we decided to give cups of hot chocolate to people who work outside: charity volunteers, mail carriers, crossing guards and trash collectors. This was such a fun day! I will never forget the crossing guard who was so overwhelmed by the simple cup of hot chocolate Garrett gave her. "No one has ever done this for me!" she exclaimed over and over.

And it was just a cup of hot chocolate.

Isn't it amazing how sometimes the simplest gestures become the biggest gifts?

That little cup of hot chocolate took all of three minutes for us to prepare. But for her, that small cup brought a little warmth to her hands and a lot of warmth to her heart.

You never know how your interactions with another person may affect the course of their life. Our world is full of so many hurting people. Sometimes the season that should bring us the greatest warmth can usher in an undercurrent of sorrow. Never underestimate the power and impact a simple one-on-one discussion or act of kindness can have. Often times, these are moments that leave lasting impressions.

The Receiver Often Became the Giver

Garrett and Grady loved visiting the police and fire station. They admire these men and women in uniform so much. During our countdown, I observed a wonderful thing. The people we gave to turned around and gave right back. For example, we toured many facilities and saw how they operated. The boys climbed on fire trucks and talked one-on-one with firemen on duty. They even tried on a bulletproof vest courtesy of a SWAT member!

In our second year of embracing a spirit of giving, we spent time at a retirement center. While there, we heard many stories from the elderly about what their childhood Christmas was like. I recall stories about favorite gifts and snowball fights, as well as meals they shared at their family table. It was then I observed another instance where the receiver became the giver. One of the residents tried to slip the kids their chocolate pudding!

Looking back through my albums of our countdowns is so heart-warming! I see many pictures of how the giver and the receiver mutually blessed each other. The expressions of the people we gave to: their smiles, tears and unmasked gratitude encourage me to keep on giving. They also remind me why we do what we do. For my family, it is a way to show how God's love will be with them always.

Personalize It

I find my kids particularly enjoy giving things that are personal to them.

Many of our gifts reflected their *favorites*. For example, the kids picked out their favorite board game and gave it to our community firefighters. Before donating to our food pantry, I took them to the grocery store and turned them loose on the canned goods aisle. They were each able to pick out their favorite fruit, vegetable and can of soup. Also, many of the care packages we sent contained a few of their favorite snacks or trinkets.

Many of their cards were written with their favorite color crayon and adorned with pictures of things they like. Ava drew typical Christmas images of angels, trees, snowmen and stockings. But, what did my youngest son, Grady, draw?

Dinosaurs.

And not just any dinosaur. We had a full-on, sharp-toothed, blood-dripping-from-its-mouth carnivore creation going on. I suppose I could have redirected him to draw something a bit more "traditional." But why? Again, it is not so much about the *what,* but the *why.* Grady's dinosaur drawings were his way of giving a piece of himself: something he found exciting, interesting and compelled to share with others.

The More We Emptied Ourselves, the Fuller We Became

"I'm tired, but filled. You'd think we'd eventually become empty from pouring ourselves into others. But, instead, I find that the more we empty ourselves, the more filled we become."

I wrote those words the day we returned home after visiting the elderly at the Veterans' Home.

We gave to these men and women on the twentieth day of our countdown the second time we embraced a spirit of giving. I so clearly remember the way the residents' faces lit up when we walked through the door. Many were gathered right at the entryway. It's like they were just hoping for someone to stop by. We made homemade ornaments to give them. I still smile when I recall the older gentleman who hung Garrett's star from the handle of his motor scooter. He looked so proud as he wheeled through the room with his new accessory.

Next, we met a man sporting a bright blue sweater and wearing a big Santa hat! He was wheelchair-bound and greeted us with a loud chorus of "Silent Night." When Ava gave him her ornament, he held her hand and sweetly kissed it before continuing on with his song.

We went room by room, visiting many people. We met a married couple that shared a room: she wore an eye patch and he had an arm lovingly draped around her. We met a man who lost both his legs. But his smile was so bright, it was nearly impossible to take our eyes off of his face.

And then there was a woman who, as she clasped Grady's hand, with tears streaming down her face, exclaimed, "I've never seen anything like this! What dear, dear children! Thank you so much for coming to see me!"

What I remember most about that night was open hands. Every time I turned, there was an outstretched palm. At first, I thought the residents were reaching for the ornaments.

But, no.

They were reaching directly for my children's hands. They wanted to feel their warmth and connect with them. And once they did, it was like they didn't want to let go. They gazed on my kids like they were little jewels. I didn't fully understand the impact of simple loving moments until then. Even though the time spent with each individual resident was fleeting, I know it was meaningful.

There's a Difference Between Good Intentions and Being Intentional

Do you ever find yourself waiting for *perfect moments*?

I received a Pizzelle Maker for Christmas one year. Pizzelles are my favorite Christmas cookie and I was so excited to finally be able to make them.

Now, you would think I instantly opened it and became a little Pizzelle-making machine. However, since I waited so long for one, I wanted to wait for a special occasion to debut my first batch. So, I waited. Then, I waited some more. After that, I kind of forgot about it. Every now and then I would open the pantry, see the Pizzelle maker on the shelf in its unopened box and think, *"Oooh, I have to make these for something special."* And then, I'd repeat the entire process.

Here's the thing about waiting for perfect moments: sometimes we become so zeroed-in on the *waiting* that we never get around to the *doing*. When we spend so much time focusing and waiting for ideal conditions or picture-perfect settings, we can end up missing opportunities. Sadly then, that idea you want to do just sits on a shelf, in its unopened box, waiting to be used.

What does this have to do with our countdown? Well, one of the lessons that really struck me during our countdown stemmed from the story I just shared. Good intentions are wonderful. Many beautiful things blossom from them. But, if we don't act on our good intentions, then we never really do anything. With this countdown, I needed my kids to understand:

You have to have more than good intentions . . . you need to be intentional.

Our countdown was the perfect vehicle for bridging the gap between good intentions and being intentional. The kids were able to take a thought and instantly put it into action.

It's Not Just About the *Give*

The moment we act upon our kind intention is wonderful.

Seeing the reaction of the person or people you give to will touch your heart in ways that will surprise you. Just be sure not to discount all the teachable moments that occur while preparing for the *give*.

Part of the challenge I faced as the kids and I gave each day was balancing time. Since many of our projects were done after school, we only had about an hour to do any creating before we went out to give. On top of that, I needed to make sure they had enough time for homework. And, somewhere in there, I needed to feed my family.

It would have been very easy for me to do all the *making* and have my kids do all the *giving*. That certainly would have solved our time issues. But on the flip side, I felt I would be robbing them of some of the values of our countdown.

Our project wasn't only about the actual *give*, but the *time* we spent preparing and putting together our gift. My kids enjoyed all the coloring, gluing, rolling and cookie cutting they did. And I valued the time I got to spend with them being fully engaged. As a mom, my attention is usually diverted in fifteen different directions. Quite the opposite occurred when we embraced a spirit of giving. When I was with them, I gave them all my attention. The time we spent together also gave us a break from *technology*. They stepped away from their game systems and gadgets, and I put down my phone.

Working together allowed us time to check in with each other. It also helped lay the groundwork to share future, intimate conversations.

I Was Better at Holding On Than Letting Go

I tend to hold on to possessions not because of the object itself, but because of the memory attached to it.

Every time I do a sweep of our attic, basement and closets, I know I'm going to find items to donate.

And I do.

But, when I think about parting with our belongings, I try to justify why a particular item should remain gathering dust:

"Well, you never know when that seventh vase might come in handy . . ."

"This was Ava's favorite 'twirling' skirt. I think she'd be upset if I donated it. I mean, I know she's ten years old and this skirt is a 3T, but really, I think we should hold on to it. Another little girl can have her turn to twirl in it next year."

"This item was a gift . . . I just can't give my gifts away. So, I'll keep it in the box instead."

And so forth.

We discovered that a giving mindset highlighted our tendency to want to hold to some things too long. It then gave us the opportunity to give away some of the things we once cherished, so someone else could make their own sweet memories.

I had the privilege of watching this idea come to life on a summer afternoon in early July.

When Ava was three-years-old, all she wanted for Christmas was a princess vanity set. In fact, it was the only item she placed on her wish list. On Christmas morning, I remember how she bolted to our Christmas tree looking for her special gift. When it came time to open presents, she immediately went for the big packages because she figured her vanity set would have to be in a big box. As the packages became smaller, I could tell she was putting on a brave face to hide her broken heart. For she slowly began to realize that her vanity set wasn't there. However, there was one more package tucked all the way behind the tree. Much to her delight, she got her beloved princess vanity set! This moment is one of my favorite Christmas morning memories I have of my kids.

Fast forward seven years and the vanity set still occupied the corner of our playroom. My daughter no longer played with it. However, one of Ava's friends, a little three-year-old neighbor girl, loved coming over to our home to play make believe with it.

One day, Ava asked me if she could surprise her young friend with the vanity set for the little girl's birthday. My initial reaction was one of hesitation. Every time I looked at the vanity set, I remembered that sweet Christmas morning from years ago. Parting with the set would be like parting with a memory. As Ava stood waiting for my answer, I suddenly realized I was right in the midst of a teachable moment. But this time, it was my daughter who was teaching me about giving.

This moment greatly touched me. This act of giving took place seven months after our twenty-five day countdown experience. It showed me that our *Embracing a Spirit of Giving* project really did impact the lives of my kids. The principles I wanted to teach them stuck! But what really moved me was that Ava's act of kindness was her initiation, not mine. One of my goals with our countdown was to equip my kids so they could teach these values to the next generation and their own children.

Well, my response to Ava was a resounding "Yes." As I watched her carry her vanity set a few houses down, I smiled. But this time, my smile wasn't evoked because of a Christmas morning memory. Instead, it was because I was so proud of my daughter's desire to pass along one of her favorite gifts so another child could enjoy the blessing.

That, and I knew in a few moments, there would be one very happy little birthday girl.

Picking Your Twenty-Five

When determining your twenty-five groups, you may be wondering, "Where do I begin?" I started by identifying and then writing down the groups that meant a lot to my kids and me. It was exciting to see how one group would springboard to the next. Before I knew it, all twenty-five days were accounted for!

When I reflect upon the people we gave to, I realize that our list is full of heroes. In fact, the groups included on our countdown list are heroes in their own way: whether it's for bravery, duty, sacrifice, service, volunteering or being an everyday hero to their family and friends. From the police officer who protects us to the postal carrier who delivers letters that keep us connected to those we hold dear, the way these individuals serve us is invaluable.

Here are a few specific groups who left very special imprints on the life of my family:

Teachers

My children have been blessed by the teachers in their lives.

They chose to honor their teachers by making them homemade Christmas cards. The kids put a lot of effort into writing their cards. I had them write down why they enjoyed their teacher and how their teacher impacted them. They then decorated their cards with various pictures. And yes, in case you are wondering, a few dinosaurs graced the cover of one child's card for his teacher.

I admire the women and men who embrace this calling. Their job requires much responsibility. Teachers do more than teach us facts and figures. They model for us how we live by demonstrating effective communication, care and correction. They have the opportunity to change lives daily and show love to those who may not receive it elsewhere. You never know what a person's home life looks like. Sometimes the classroom is where a child is built up the most. Teachers can nurture children and help them develop by the skills they teach, and by the example they set.

I am blessed to be one whose life was touched because of the time teachers invested in me.

Our Church

I am grateful for our church and the people who come along side me, helping reinforce what is taught in our home.

My family had the honor of calling SouthField Community Church in Channahon, IL, and now Friendship Community Church in Mount Juliet, TN, our church home. In these two homes, we are part of a family of believers who help us develop a real relationship with God and grow in our desire to be more like Christ.

I am so appreciative of the people in my kids' lives who help instill the morals and values I hold dear. They include pastors, Sunday school teachers, small group leaders, prayer partners, ministry leaders, volunteers, etc. The time these individuals invest in my kids is not taken lightly. I love hearing about the stories, songs and Bible verses they learn. I pray that these truths will take root in the heart of my children. I also pray they will continue to encounter individuals who will nurture these truths throughout their lives.

The kids and I acknowledged some of the individuals in our church by giving them homemade packets to make *cups of good cheer* (hot chocolate!). We filled baggies with cocoa and marshmallows. Then we crushed up peppermint candies and placed them on top. This way, the kids' Sunday School teachers could enjoy a sweet cup at their convenience. It was a simple and cute gift!

Nurses

I have a lot of respect for people who serve in the nursing field. It is the friendly faces of nurses you see as you undergo medical treatment. Their steady hands hold your own shaking ones as you go through procedures and tests. Their reassuring voices can help soothe your fears and pain. They are compassionate people with a heart for others and their well-being. They sacrifice days many would consider "sacred" to their own family for the sake of others—weekends and holidays.

I contacted a family member who is in the nursing field for ideas on how to give to these sweet heroes. It turns out that nurses not only appreciate goodies, but they are in constant need of pens. I never would have thought of that on my own! So off we went with a plate of English toffee squares and a handful of pens to our local hospital. Getting advice from people who work in the field you are giving to is so helpful. There is nothing like receiving firsthand information from people who know.

Firefighters

When I think about *heroes*, I count firefighters among them. They continually risk their lives for others and their dedication to their community is admirable. I recall September 11, 2001 and am struck by the number of men and women who lost their lives because of their great love for other people. They selflessly raced into burning buildings to save someone they didn't know. The way they were willing to lay down their own life to save another one is indeed a great form of love.

One year we showed our appreciation to our local firefighters by making them a gingerbread house. The kids had a blast with this! They loved placing little candies and gumdrops all along the gingerbread. But, I had to keep my eye on them. There were moments when I wasn't sure if they were putting more candy on the gingerbread house or into their mouths! Their favorite part was squeezing and spreading the icing all over their masterpiece. I don't think I have ever seen so much icing dripping from a rooftop! It was a fun project to make and an even better one to eat.

Mentors and Coaches

Do you or your kids have a mentor or coach? Is there someone who helps you develop a specific skill, tutor you with your studies, guide your answers to questions or advise you in the choices you make? These people give by helping us realize our fullest potential and to be all we are capable of becoming.

My kids made ornaments that symbolized how their mentor was influencing them. For example, Ava made a musical note for her choir teacher. These little tokens of appreciation were examples of how these special people enriched the lives of my children.

It's Not Always Easy

I just shared stories about people who were easy for us to give to. What about the people who hurt us or are considered society's misfits? Are they to be denied the joy brought by an act of kindness?

There are people who manage getting on your nerves with a look. They make you feel tired just thinking of them, and challenge your ability to control your tongue and temper. They may berate, belittle or devalue you. No one deserves this treatment.

Be honest now . . .

Isn't it easier to give to those who make us feel all warm and fuzzy inside?

Yet, when we think about giving to people who add misery to our day, we tighten our fist and draw back the arm we should be extending.

Remember how I shared how giving should be unconditional—with no strings attached?

We shouldn't just give to people we enjoy being with; we also need to give to those who are difficult to love. Our standard for giving should not be *do they deserve it*? Instead, it should stem from a place of grace.

Giving is always easier when you feel valued and respected by those you interact with. It is challenging to give to *difficult* people in your life. We can get a great sense of personal satisfaction when we give to people, regardless of who they are. It doesn't have to be much. If you're looking for a place to start, then begin with a sincere, "Good morning."

The Difference Between *Have to* and *Get to*

I am a list person.

I like making lists, but even more, I love crossing items off them when they are complete. It allows me to see what I've accomplished and what remains to be done.

However, I had to make a concentrated effort not to let our countdown become part of the checklist of things I *had to* do during my day. I understand how busy the Christmas season is and how you can feel pulled in just about every direction— like a big piece of taffy. Why, there were days when I felt like I needed to schedule myself a bathroom break! I remember one day, in particular, as I ran through my daily list, finding myself prefacing everything with *have to*. It hit me suddenly, that this was a terrible way to think. *Have to* makes me feel like a slave to my schedule. So, I knew a little reframing was in order. I began replacing *have to* with *get to*. First of all, when I say I *get to* do something as opposed to *have to*, I instantly feel more anticipation and excitement. Also, *get to* moves me away from a powerless position when it comes to how I view my schedule. It empowers me to declare ownership of my time.

When it comes to my children, I don't want giving to be a *have to* or a requirement. It should be from a personal willingness within. I want their desire to give to be year round, and not confined to a specific season.

But, I'm SO Busy . . .

I'm Busy.

You're Busy.

Everybody's Busy.

Now, that we've cleared that up, let's move on.

Seriously though, I understand what it feels like to be overwhelmed trying to accomplish many things at once. And I swear there are some people who must have an extra hour in their day and just don't admit it.

Personally, I don't think I really know what it's like operating without my plate full. Perhaps I should take a cue from my eating habits. I'm a grazer. I don't like sitting down to full plates; I prefer picking throughout the day. Yet, when it comes to life, it's like I grab the biggest ladle of things to do and heap it on myself.

I could sit here and share all the reasons why I'm busy. And some of these reasons are quite legitimate. I could explain that as a mother of three, I am constantly on the go. I'm involved in several good things, but when added together, they divert my attention in many different directions. My goodness, when I add to the mix my tendency to take on so many things (because I really do enjoy helping . . . and I have a hard time saying "no"), I often find myself trying to balance a plate literally overflowing with commitments.

Yep, I sure am busy.

But, you know what I learned during our countdown?

Full plates are quite costly. And I needed to do a better job evaluating the price I pay for my plate. Because quite honestly, when I hear myself say "I'm so busy," I feel like all I'm really doing is trying to justify what my full plate costs me.

It's ironic how giving is often accompanied with a sweetness knowing we did something good. Yet, at the same time, also reveals areas of our life where we may be selfish: whether it is with our time, resources, finances, love, affection or encouragement.

One of the hardest discoveries I made about myself was when I thought back and recalled not the ways I gave, but the times I didn't. When I reflected on these moments, the phrase, *"I'm so busy,"* was tied to many of them. And truthfully, my *"I'm so busy"* rang hollow because it was my way of making an excuse for something I just didn't want to do.

Twenty-five days can seem like a lot.

But, is it really?

If we can't think of one kind thing to do or say each day during the countdown, then we have lost sight of one of the most beautiful purposes we have: our call to love others.

So, you may be wondering . . .

Why pick one of the traditionally busiest times of the year and add to it?

Simple. If we can take some time each day during one of the busiest times of the year, then how much easier will it be to continue spreading kindness when life is at a slower pace?

So, I have good news for those with busy schedules! In the suggestion list you will find varying ways to reach out and give. As you will discover, some ideas take a moment; others entail more activity. Some suggestions require you to plan and schedule ahead of time; others can be done spur-of-the-moment. There are ways to love by going out in the community and ways to show love from your home.

You may find ideas you want to do, but can't fit into your busy Christmas season schedule. Or, you may see something on the list that you really wanted to get to, but ran out of days. Don't be discouraged!

Giving is not confined to one specific season. If summertime is a less busy time for you, then consider having a "Christmas in July." Or, if your down time falls during a different time of the year, embrace your spirit of giving countdown then.

Set aside a time period of twenty-five days and watch how you and your family change.

"Mommy, I want . . . !"

Ready to make our donations.

Rolling out dough for gingerbread men. I love Grady's chef hat!

We made star ornaments using wooden craft sticks. They were simple, yet fun to make. Cookie cutters also make great stencils!

Our Advent calendar

A stop on our "Quarter Crusade."
We had a blast strategically
placing quarters around town!

Making Pizzelles . . . yum!

Creating Christmas ornaments
for our local hospital.

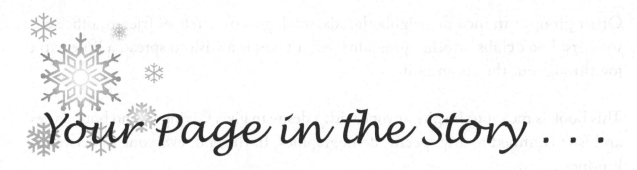

Your Page in the Story . . .

Throughout the course of the countdown, many people asked where they could get "the book," so they could do our project. I was very humbled by the question and my reply was simple, "There is no book. The idea was a *gift* that existed in my heart and came to life as we put it into action."

The question continued to linger in my mind. If I were to write "the book," what would it look like?

My answer was found in a wonderful quote by Benjamin Franklin:

"Tell me and I forget. Teach me and I remember. Involve me and I learn."

These words inspired me to write this book. However, I wanted to do more than tell my family's story or simply share the lessons we learned along the way. I hoped to inspire others into action.

If one family's story could inspire others, what would a home, neighborhood, community or world look like when many people partner together to make a difference in the lives of others?

The next section is your opportunity to get involved.

I have shared my experience of a twenty-five day countdown. Now, it is your turn.

Your *Spirit of Giving* countdown can be embraced in a variety of ways. It can be done solo, with a friend or a group of people. Perhaps you are a parent or grandparent doing this with a child, a teacher wanting to do a class project, a retired individual sharing time with others, or a Church ministering to their community.

Other groups can include neighborhoods, small groups, circle of friends, office co-workers, book clubs or other programs. All it takes is a wish to spread a little extra joy throughout the community.

This book is meant to inspire anyone with a desire to give. Giving has no boundaries and isn't confined to any specific demographics. In the end, everyone understands kindness.

I've often heard that Christmas and Easter are the two times, more than any other during the year, when people attend church. What if this year, your *Christmas Service* isn't just a single event where people gather together at one place, at one time, on one day? What if instead of only attending a service, we went out and *served*?

A Story Meant for Such a Time as This . . .

If you asked me what I wanted to be when I grew up, my five-year-old self would have answered,

"A teacher."

In my own way, it is who I have become.

I get to teach my kids every day. I try to take the things I value and hold sacred and tuck it away in their hearts. I want them to believe and have faith in things they cannot see. I long for them to experience a childhood laced with imagination, hopes and dreams. I pray they grow up feeling secure in my love, knowing even when they fall short, I will always be there ready to help them stand tall. I am a mother who is doing the best she can to teach her children how to live.

When I look at my children, I am so proud of who they are and who they are becoming. My parents passed down a legacy of giving which I share with my children today. My hope is they will one day share this legacy with their children and generations to come.

This is why I created this countdown and share my story with you today.

Call me idealistic, but I really believe every act of kindness, no matter how simple in nature, can change a heart. When hearts change, our world changes. The values and lessons we instill into our children today will influence future generations.

We are not promised tomorrow, but we are given today. What we do with it is our gift to others.

My friends . . .

May you dwell in love as you journey through these next twenty-five days. May you find joy in unexpected places, happiness in sweet moments, and a gentle peace beyond understanding. I pray you create beautiful memories with each life you touch, and embrace a spirit of giving not only for a season, but for a lifetime.

Kelly Christine

"Embracing a Spirit of Giving," Christmas 2010

When someone has been given much, much will be required; and when someone has been entrusted with much, even much more will be required.
—Luke 12:48

Thankful for this reminder. Thankful to be entrusted.
Thankful for the opportunity to give.

Create Something Lasting . . .

Now, it's your turn!

I daily chronicled my family's adventures as we journeyed though our countdown. Each day, I highlighted our tender moments, mishaps, valuable lessons and other teachable moments we experienced. I took pictures every day of the kids prepping their *give*, sharing their gifts and loving in action.

This section is designed in a similar way. Each day you can write about your experience. You can include pictures, your account of the event, or something sweet another person said. You can also keep memorable tokens or items that illustrate how the day impacted and blessed both the receiver, and you, the giver. You decide who and how you would like to give each day. Remember, this is your story! You can tell it any way you like.

Throughout this countdown you will encounter many moments to tuck within your heart and the confines of these pages. This book is your place to store up these memories, keeping them readily available to reflect on and share throughout the years.

I've included our countdown list and the different ways we gave. However, I expanded each category to give you other ideas ranging in amounts of required time and resources. You can use my suggestions or they may inspire ideas of your own. If you feel led in a certain way, go with it!

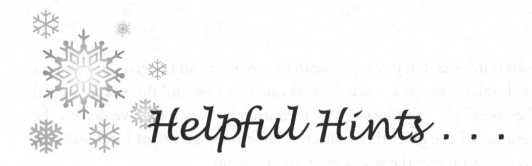

Helpful Hints . . .

Plan ahead

- If you plan out your week in advance, you can do your shopping all at once. You decide how involved of a *give* you want to do each day. If your weekdays are very busy, then select activities that don't require much preparation. If you have more time on the weekends, arrange to do more involved *gives* then.
- Call facilities ahead of time. See what days and times they are open or welcome visitors. I don't know why, but I continually think the post office is open later than it is. There were many times when we made it in and out of a place right before closing time. Also, verify what age people need to be to serve.
- Select groups that coincide with your family's weekly schedule. For example, if your child attends piano lessons on a certain day of the week, then choose that day to honor her mentor or teacher.

Do your research

- I still remember the day I took the kids on the tollway with the intention of giving hot chocolate to toll booth workers. Turns out they are unable to accept items from people. Oops . . .
- If you are planning on baking, make sure the people you are baking for can accept homemade goodies. Due to concerns about contamination, some facilities can only accept pre-packaged food.
- Due to privacy laws, many facilities such as retirement centers and nursing homes will not allow you to take pictures of the residents. If you want a picture of a *give* that involves such a facility, take pictures in the lobby or outside the facility.

Pace yourself

This countdown is intended to give joy to both the receiver and the giver. If you find yourself stressed, take it down a notch. This is not a contest and there is no medal or prize for the "best" gift. Kindness is not measured by how much we do. It's the heart and intention of the giver that matters. Remember, an act of kindness that seems small to us, can mean the world to another person.

Be flexible

So, you don't have time to don an apron, get out the rolling pin and make cookies from scratch?

No problem! If you still want the baking experience, but are short on time, pick up a container of precut cookies, pop them in the oven and *voila!* . . . instant treat.

No time to even wait for that oven to preheat?

Again, no worries! Buy a package of cookies and stick a cute post-it note on top.

One of the best pieces of advice I can give is to adjust and adapt. If an idea looks interesting to you, but is not one you can fully undertake, then alter it. There are many ways you can meaningfully give and still have time to take care of your family's needs.

When you encounter a bump along the way, just roll with it. Don't freak out. Just detour, and go a different direction. One year, we had "Giving to Our Environment" as the focus of our day. Our plan was to go and pick up litter in our neighborhood. And then it snowed . . . a lot. So, we put on hats and gloves and did what we could. Later, I ended up talking to the kids about the importance of energy conservation. The pictures of the kids all bundled up are great and it's become a fun story to recall and tell to others.

<u>Have Fun</u>

At the back of the book is a "Countdown Calendar." It's a fun tool you can use to visualize your twenty-five day journey. One of the things my kids and I really enjoyed was the suspense and excitement of each new day. The kids never knew what was coming next! They had to wait until the next morning to find out our daily *give*.

25-Day Countdown List and Suggestions

1. ### The Military

   - Send a care package overseas
   - Visit a Veterans' Home
   - Place flowers on a soldier's unmarked grave
   - Adopt a soldier
   - Buy a pre-paid phone card
   - Make a meal or treat for a soldier's spouse or family

2. ### Global Missions

   - Donate money
   - Sponsor a child
   - Fill a jar with coins to give to a specific mission project
   - Have a lemonade (or hot chocolate!) stand and donate the proceeds

3. ### Day Care Workers, Babysitters and Caregivers

   - Give a gift card
   - Buy a set of movie tickets
   - Give a stocking filled with some of your kids' favorite items

4. ### The Environment

   - Start recycling
   - Make a plan to conserve energy and resources in your home

- Pick up litter
- Get seeds started to grow outside in the spring

5. *Firefighters*

- Buy a favorite board game or card game
- Give a Gingerbread House kit . . . a fun project and treat all in one
- Fill a jar with candy . . . a sweet way to honor them
- Buy or make pizza for the crew

6. *Servers* (restaurant staff, bellhops, taxi drivers, hair dressers etc . . .)

- Tip your regular amount and then give extra
- Compliment service to management
- Give a gift card

7. *Medical Professionals* (doctors, dentists, physical therapists, etc . . .)

- Bring a plate of baked goodies . . . always a welcome sight
- Treat them with chocolate dipped pretzel sticks
- Surprise them with a flower arrangement
- Bring a box of chicken soup and crackers
- Give a fruit basket
- Write a note of thanks

8. *Neighbors*

- Bake a plate of goodies to share
- Buy a plant for their yard
- Walk over and visit for a while
- Bring a meal . . . especially for a sick neighbor
- Mow their lawn or shovel their driveway

9. _Those Who Work Outside_ (crossing guards, Salvation Army volunteers, trash collectors, etc . . .)

- Give cups of hot chocolate to warm them up
- Give a gift card so they can buy their own _cup of good cheer_
- Give a pack of gum, thanking them for the smile they bring you
- Give hand-warmers
- Hand out water bottles

10. _Shelters and Local Missions_

- Go through your belongings and donate clothing and household goods
- Have your kids donate a toy
- Donate your automobile

11. _Less Fortunate Children_

- Go through the ads and select a toy for a child
- Pay for the lunch of a less fortunate child at your school
- Donate books or supplies

12. _Coaches and Mentors_

- Write a note telling what they mean to you and about the impact they are having or have had on your life
- Give a Poinsettia or another plant
- Make them a homemade certificate of appreciation

13. _Co-Workers and Bosses_

- Acknowledge or compliment a job well done
- Give a smile
- Bake or bring in a treat
- Trade shifts with a co-worker in need

14. *Nurses*

- Bake cookies for the nurses at your hospital or care clinic
- Donate pens
- Buy a pedicure for your favorite nurse
- Give bath salts
- Energize them with trail mix

15. *Postal Carriers*

- Make a paper ornament they can attach to their mail truck
- Give them a cup of hot chocolate
- Meet them at your mailbox and thank them for bringing your mail
- Give them a water bottle

16. *Teachers*

- Have your child make a card telling why they love and appreciate their teacher . . . you make one too
- Give a gift certificate for their favorite store or restaurant
- Bring them an apple
- Volunteer in the classroom or offer to read to the class

17. *Animals*

- Pick up a box of treats or toys for an animal shelter
- Consider adopting a pet ☺
- Make a birdhouse out of a milk carton
- String popcorn and decorate your bushes or trees
- Buy a loaf of bread to feed the birds or ducks
- Walk someone's dog
- Volunteer at an animal boarding house

18. _Pastors, Spiritual Influences and Sunday School Teachers_

- Put together a hot chocolate care package filled with cocoa, marshmallows and peppermint
- Make a card that tells the person what they mean to you
- Buy your pastor a book
- Make them an ornament

19. _The Homeless and Hungry_

- Volunteer to serve at your local food pantry
- Select items from your pantry to donate to a food shelter
- Volunteer at a homeless shelter
- Donate blankets and coats
- Go to the grocery store and let your kids pick out their favorite canned goods to donate
- Make a care package full of toiletries to give to the homeless
- Buy a newspaper from a homeless person

20. _The Elderly_

- Visit a retirement center
- Make ornaments to hand out to the residents of a nursing home
- Sing carols
- Visit a person who is shut-in
- Donate non-slip socks to residents in a retirement center

21. _Friends_

- Prepare a meal for another family
- Offer to watch a couple's kids so they can enjoy a date night
- Purchase a magazine subscription for a friend's hobby
- Treat a friend to lunch

22. *The Sick*

- Make ornaments to decorate the pediatric wing of a hospital
- Donate to a cause or charity dear to you
- Keep someone company as they undergo medical treatment
- Provide transportation to a doctor appointment
- Bring them a meal

23. *Police Officers*

- Bring a box of cookies to a police station (they usually can't accept homemade food due to contamination concerns)
- Drop off a box of doughnuts or bagels
- Make a donation to a police officer memorial

24. *Random Acts of Kindness*

- "Quarter Crusade" Place quarters in parking meters and candy jars. Tape them to photo booths, massage chairs, laundromats, vending machines, arcade games, rides, etc . . . this was my kids' favorite act of kindness
- Pay for the order of the vehicle behind you in a drive-thru line
- Return a grocery cart for someone
- Hold open a door for another person
- "25 Stamps" Send a letter each day throughout the countdown to people you know . . . a welcome change from the usual bills found in a mailbox
- Buy a cookie coupon so a child waiting in line to see Santa can have a treat to enjoy

25. *Celebrating Christ and Honoring Family*

- Read a biblical Christmas story together
- Write each member of your family a special letter
- Have a family movie night
- Eat dinner together as a family at your table
- Play a game together

Other "Gifts" . . .

- Let someone go ahead of you in line
- Donate blood
- Give a container of cookies to your bus driver
- Decorate a Christmas tree for someone else
- Fill a stocking and give it to another person
- Look someone in the eye and smile
- Send a care package to a college student . . . they love snacks for late night studying
- Donate books to your local library
- Give a hug
- Fill up another person's gas tank
- Tutor a child
- Write a poem for another person
- Donate hair

Embracing a Spirit of
Giving Scrapbook

Date:

What did you do?

Who did you do it with?

What did you learn?

Who did you meet?

Special memories or moments

Date:

What did you do?

Who did you do it with?

What did you learn?

Where did you go?

How did you make a difference today?

Date:

What did you do?

Who did you do it with?

What did you learn?

What surprised you?

Did today's experience inspire you to make any personal changes?

Date:

What did you do?

Who did you do it with?

What did you learn?

Would you do this again?

Today, you blessed someone with your giving. How were you blessed in return?

Pictures and Keepsakes

Date:

What did you do?

Who did you do it with?

What did you learn?

What made you laugh?

What was your favorite part about today?

Pictures and Keepsakes

Date:

What did you do?

Who did you do it with?

What did you learn?

Who did you meet?

Special memories or moments

Pictures and Keepsakes

Date:

What did you do?

Who did you do it with?

What did you learn?

Where did you go?

How did you make a difference today?

Date:

What did you do?

Who did you do it with?

What did you learn?

What surprised you?

Did today's experience inspire you to make any personal changes?

Date:

What did you do?

Who did you do it with?

What did you learn?

Would you do this again?

Today, you blessed someone with your giving. How were you blessed in return?

Pictures and Keepsakes

Date:

What did you do?

Who did you do it with?

What did you learn?

What made you laugh?

What was your favorite part about today?

Pictures and Keepsakes

Date:

What did you do?

Who did you do it with?

What did you learn?

Who did you meet?

Special memories or moments

Pictures and Keepsakes

Date:

What did you do?

Who did you do it with?

What did you learn?

Where did you go?

How did you make a difference today?

Date:

What did you do?

Who did you do it with?

What did you learn?

What surprised you?

Did today's experience inspire you to make any personal changes?

Date:

What did you do?

Who did you do it with?

What did you learn?

Would you do this again?

Today, you blessed someone with your giving. How were you blessed in return?

Pictures and Keepsakes

Date:

What did you do?

Who did you do it with?

What did you learn?

What made you laugh?

What was your favorite part about today?

Date:

What did you do?

Who did you do it with?

What did you learn?

Who did you meet?

Special memories or moments

Date:

What did you do?

Who did you do it with?

What did you learn?

Where did you go?

How did you make a difference today?

Date:

What did you do?

Who did you do it with?

What did you learn?

What surprised you?

Did today's experience inspire you to make any personal changes?

Date:

What did you do?

Who did you do it with?

What did you learn?

Would you do this again?

Today, you blessed someone with your giving. How were you blessed in return?

Date:

What did you do?

Who did you do it with?

What did you learn?

What made you laugh?

What was your favorite part about today?

Date:

What did you do?

Who did you do it with?

What did you learn?

Who did you meet?

Special memories or moments

Date:

What did you do?

Who did you do it with?

What did you learn?

Where did you go?

How did you make a difference today?

Date:

What did you do?

Who did you do it with?

What did you learn?

What surprised you?

Did today's experience inspire you to make any personal changes?

Date:

What did you do?

Who did you do it with?

What did you learn?

Would you do this again?

Today, you blessed someone with your giving. How were you blessed in return?

Pictures and Keepsakes

Date:

What did you do?

Who did you do it with?

What did you learn?

What made you laugh?

What was your favorite part about today?

Pictures and Keepsakes

Countdown Calendar